Egyptian Soups
HOT AND COLD

John Feeney

Egyptian Soups
HOT AND COLD

With photographs by the author

The American University in Cairo Press

Cairo New York

ISBN-10: 977 416 019 3
ISBN-13: 978 977 416 019 6
Dar el Kutub No. 23756/05

Designed by Andrea El-Akshar
Printed in Egypt

Contents

Introduction

These seventeen original soup recipes were conceived in Cairo and used by myself and my faithful cook Shehata for over thirty years. Diligent in the extreme, and a wonderful cook, Shehata—also known as Mohamed—came from a Nubian village close to Ramesses II's 3,500-year-old temples at Abu Simbel. He had hoped, when he retired, to return to his beloved Nubia, but Nubia vanished under the waters of the Aswan High Dam, and after working with me for twenty-five years, Shehata died peacefully, a good and faithful man.

To make a really good, delectable soup can take as much time and care as the making of a meat or fish dish. There should be nothing haphazard about its preparation. Rarely can the proverbial 'stock pot' contribute much in the way of a worthwhile stock. After a day or two of simmering on the stove, a stock becomes a sour, dull liquid of little culinary use. Instead, a separate collection of vegetable, meat, fish, and fruit juices, stored individually in glass jars in the refrigerator, can prove to be of much more value. Otherwise, it is best to prepare fresh stock as required.

And remember, a hot soup must be hot, very hot. All over the world, I often have to send the soup back to be heated up. It doesn't matter if you prefer your soup lukewarm or tepid—a terrible thought, but if you do, then start off with the soup very hot and let it linger for a few minutes until it reaches your desired temperature.

Likewise, the usual flat, wide soup plate is an abomination and should never be used. Within a minute, a soup served in one of these awful plates has become cold. It is much better to use a soup bowl, which keeps soup hot to the last spoonful.

Note: 'Cup' in these recipes means an English teacup, which holds the same as a 125g carton of yogurt.

Hot
Soups

Mastic, *mistka* in Arabic, a somewhat mysterious substance, is one of the key ingredients in Mohamed's Mystic Arabian Broth. The white resinous tears of gum are exuded from the bark of a small evergreen shrub *(Pistacia lentiscus)* that grows mainly along the Hadramawt coast of southern Arabia, and in Turkey. It is widely used medicinally by people of the east as a 'nervous calmative,' as a tea and coffee infusion, and in cooking. As one might expect, it is said to be an aphrodisiac. I wouldn't dream of trying it, if I were you, but dare I tell you that in Malaysia they make a wild concoction of mastic, opium, honey, and aromatic herbs. Sometimes, when we had guests in Heliopolis, as a special treat Mohamed would use mastic to per-fume the coffee cups. He would place a few grains of it on a thin tray, warm it over a gas jet, and then place the coffee cups over the fuming mastic for a few minutes before turning up the cups and filling them with his rich black Turkish coffee. The mastic fumes imparted a delightful aroma. Here is the original recipe for Mohamed's Mystic Arabian Broth, to which the mastic gives a beautiful whiff of incense.

Mohamed's Mystic Arabian Broth

Aphrodisiac

A light soup sometimes possessing a fragrance akin to frankincense

This is a good soup to make after boiling a whole chicken, which should be done in salted water with two halved onions, three pearls of garlic, three bay leaves, four *habbahan* (cardamom) pods, two carrots, and a teaspoon of thyme—all necessary to make a strong chicken stock. To make this soup with chicken bouillon cubes will not work.

Ingredients for 6 servings

9 cups of rich chicken stock, strained; remove all the fat when chilled
2 cups of finely chopped lamb pieces
3 medium-sized onions, halved, or two cups of chopped leeks
3 pearls of garlic, peeled and uncut
6 pods of habbahan (cardamom)
3 medium bay leaves
1 teaspoon tears of mastic
1/2 cup cooked white rice
Salt, white pepper, a pinch of red cayenne pepper, and a big squeeze of lime juice

Habbahan

Habbahan in Arabic, *Hibiscus abelmochus* in Latin, and cardamom in English, this aromatic spice is related to the ginger family. It is said to have come from the Cardamom Hills of India. For centuries, it was one of the precious spices carried to the Middle East by Arab mariners and caravan traders. But long before this, the Ebers Papyrus, a pharmacological treatise written about 1550 BC, records that the ancient Egyptians were using cardamom in their medicines, in cosmetic ointments, in perfumes, and in fumigation and embalming procedures. Today in Egypt, Saudi Arabia, and Kuwait, cardamom is used widely in rice dishes, tea and coffee. And what a perfume fills the house when *habbahan* is infusing.

Method

1. Boil the meat in two cups of the chicken stock for about 45 minutes, or until tender.
2. Boil the onions, garlic, habbahan, and bay leaves in the remaining chicken stock for 25 minutes. Then strain the stock, discarding seasonings.
3. Add the cooked lamb and its liquid.
4. Skim the broth.
5. Dissolve the mastic in the soup while simmering.
6. Add the cooked rice.
7. Season with salt, white pepper, and red cayenne pepper to taste.
8. Serve immediately, adding a few liberal squeezes of lime juice.

Guava

Highly perfumed, resembling a pale yellow pear, the guava has cream or rose-colored flesh, which surrounds the large mass of very hard seeds. A much-traveled fruit, it is related to the cinnamon tree of Sri Lanka, the clove of Zanzibar, and the eucalyptus tree of Australia. So what wouldn't be highly perfumed, with these three exotic trees in the family? But how the guava gained these relatives, goodness only knows.

Ginger
A spice to dream about

Ginger, *Zingiber officinale*, *ganzabil* in
Arabic, has, since the days of antiquity,
always had a 'reputation.' And indeed,
to this day in Egypt it is not always
considered polite to even mention *ganzabil*. In his little manual "The Perfumed
Garden," written in the fourteenth century,
Sheikh Omar ibn Muhammad al-Nafzawi
makes several suggestions for using
ginger. What really packs a punch, the
sheikh says, is a concoction of powdered
ginger, nutmeg, and mastic mixed with
honey, "to be taken in small doses daily."
The sheikh's little manual is kept under
lock and key by the librarian of the
London Library—I had quite a job getting
it out to read.

In medieval times, Cairo merchants
made their fortunes importing vast
amounts of ginger from southeast Asia
and exporting it to Europe, down the
Nile to Venetian and Genoese galleys
waiting at Alexandria.

Fresh root ginger is used in abundance in several of the cold soups later
in this book.

Cream of Guava and Ginger Soup

Ambrosial*

Until this moment (for soon everyone will be making it), no one has ever talked about a recipe for a hot Cream of Guava and Ginger Soup, not to be confused with our Iced Guava Soup, which is quite different. This delicious fruity, slightly tart soup is a highly original recipe.

Ingredients for 4 servings

2 chicken bouillon cubes

1 cup hot water

3 cups of fresh guava pulp (carefully peel off the large central seed mass)

1 tablespoon dried mint, powdered in the fingers

1 tablespoon freshly grated ginger

3 cups Greek- or Turkish-style yogurt, beaten to a creamy consistency

1 tablespoon white sugar

1/4 teaspoon red cayenne pepper

White pepper, no salt

1/2 cup light cream

Juice of 1 green lime, or half a lemon

Method

1. Dissolve the chicken cubes in a cup of hot water.
2. Stir in the guava pulp (reserving half a cup).
3. Mix in the dried mint and grated ginger.
4. Bring to a simmer, but do not boil, for five minutes.
5. Stir 5 to 6 spoonfuls of the hot guava mixture into the beaten yogurt. Then add to the rest of the hot guava in the pot.
6. Add sugar, red pepper, and white pepper. Do not salt.
7. Simmer for five more minutes. Do not allow to boil.
8. Stir in the cream, lime or lemon juice, and the remaining half cup of guava pulp.
9. Keep hot and serve with thin Melba toast, crisp 'aysh shami, or warm cheese straws.

*Ambrosial—meaning 'divine,' 'food of the gods.'

Delice Persan Chaud

Pomegranate Soup

Ambrosial and Aphrodisiac

Punica granatum in Latin, *rumman* in Arabic, the pomegranate is one of the symbolic fruits of ancient Egypt. Paintings of pomegranate fruits and flowers were used to decorate the walls of Egyptian palaces, temples, and tombs. Ramesses III grew pomegranates in his Delta gardens and distributed them on a regular basis to priests in the temples. In more recent ages, images of pomegranate flowers and fruit have been used to adorn the vestments of Coptic priests.

This recipe is quite different from the Iced Pomegranate Soup—Delice Persan Froid.

How to extract the seeds and juice from the whole pomegranate

At first glance, on seeing the densely packed ruby-red seeds glistening inside a halved pomegranate, it may seem a daunting task to extract the juice. Nothing could be simpler:

1. Wash and halve each pomegranate, cutting across at the center, or meridian, not top to bottom.
2. Hold one half face down in the palm of the hand over a collecting bowl.
3. In the right hand take a small hammer or heavy-handled object. Sharply strike the outer skin of the halved pomegranate, first in the center, then knocking around the sides. Keep hitting the halved pomegranate sharply. In less than 30 seconds all the ripe pomegranate seeds will have fallen out into your hand and dropped into the bowl below. The few remaining seeds can be pushed out with the fingers.
4. Remove any white pith that has fallen out with the seeds.
5. Place the loose seeds in a blender, or a moulinette. Blend at liquidizing speed for 20 seconds.
6. Strain off the juice into a glass or enamel container.
7. Return the seed residue remaining in the strainer into the blender. Pour in 1 cup of cold water and blend again for a few seconds. Pour back into the strainer and press hard with a wooden spoon, extracting the rich remaining juice, which can greatly enhance the texture and flavor of the soup.

Note: Ravishing and glamorous as the seeds look, pomegranate juice is an extremely powerful liquid. When some kinds of metal containers come into contact with raw, uncooked pomegranate juice, the juice turns black within minutes, especially when heat is applied. Therefore, *never* use an uncoated iron, copper, or steel pot to make this soup. Always use a stainless steel or enameled pot.

Ingredients for 6 servings

1 medium onion, very finely chopped
3 cubes beef bouillon
3 bay leaves
1 teaspoon dried thyme, powdered in the fingers
2 tablespoons dried mint, powdered in the fingers
1 tablespoon white sugar
10 cm (4 inches) of cinnamon bark—never use powdered cinnamon, which quickly becomes stale
2 cups cold water
6 cups of fresh pomegranate juice extracted from approximately 2 kilograms of fruit
1 tablespoon dried tarragon, powdered in the fingers
2 cups beaten unsalted Greek- or Turkish-style yogurt
Juice and grated zest of 1 sweet orange
1 teaspoon white pepper
4 tablespoons cognac (optional)
1 teaspoon freshly grated nutmeg
No salt
1 cut lime

Method

1. Put the onion, beef cubes, bay leaves, thyme, mint, sugar, and cinnamon into 2 cups of cold water and simmer for 5 minutes.
2. Add 5 of the 6 cups of fresh pomegranate juice and powdered tarragon leaves and warm slightly. Never let the pomegranate juice boil.
3. Stir the warm pomegranate liquid, half a cup at a time, into the beaten yogurt.
4. Stir in the grated orange zest and juice, the white pepper, and the optional cognac.
5. Remove the cinnamon bark.
6. Slowly bring to a simmer, using a heat-diffuser beneath the pot.
7. Just before serving, add the 6th cup of pomegranate juice, the nutmeg, and a squeeze of fresh lime juice. Keep hot.
8. Serve with toasted 'aysh shami, Melba toast or, best of all, warm cheese straws.

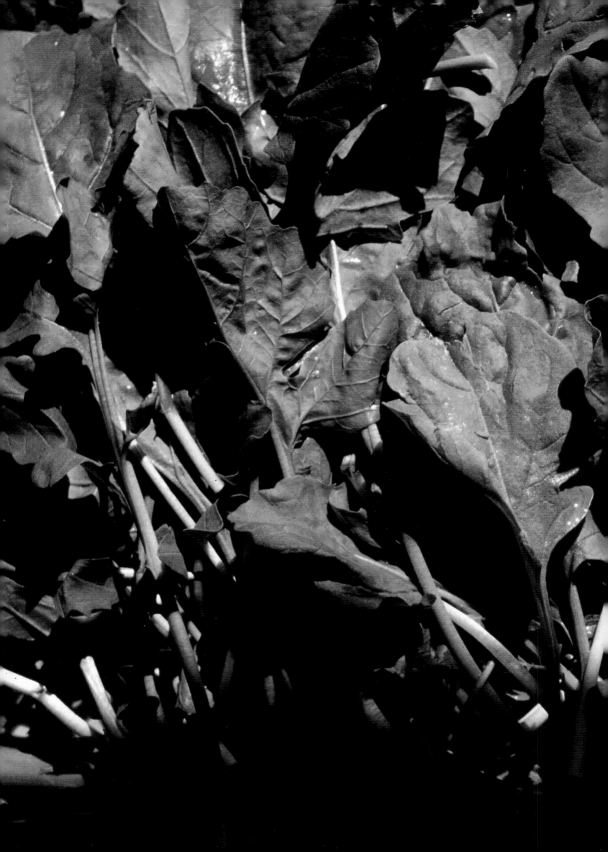

Gargir Soup

Aphrodisiac

Some soups can take hours to prepare, but if all the ingredients are ready at hand, this one is very simple and takes no more than 30 minutes to make.

Indigenous to North Africa, *gargir*—rocket or arugula *(Eruca sativa)*—is a common green herb that has been used in Egypt for generations. The fellaheen, the farmers of Egypt, swear by *gargir*. For millennia they have eaten sprigs of *gargir* with their midday meal in the fields, along with 'aysh baladi (local coarse wheat bread), green onions, and a glass of water. Sometimes called 'Egyptian watercress,' it does possess certain affinities with *cresson*. It is usually eaten fresh, as a salad, with a squeeze of lime and oil, and I doubt if anyone until now has ever made a soup out of it. But try, and you will be delighted. In fact, along with our Cream of *Sabanikh* (Spinach Soup), because of its aphrodisiac attributes, this is a Soup of Delights.

If this original recipe should ever catch on, it could become another very 'Egyptian' soup, for in a way it is akin to the famous Egyptian *mulukhiya*

Ingredients for 6 servings

4 large bunches fresh gargir (cut gargir does not stay fresh for more than a day or two)
3 medium-sized onions, roughly chopped
2 cups peeled and boiled potatoes, roughly cut
6 peeled and quartered pearls of garlic
1 large handful shabat (dill) stripped from the stalk
2 large handfuls fresh kuzbara (coriander) leaves
2 tablespoons ground kuzbara (coriander) seed
1 tablespoon unsalted butter
2 beef cubes
6 cups boiling water
2 cups beaten Greek- or Turkish-style yogurt
Salt, black pepper, and a good dash of red pepper
6 slices white bread and cooking oil for making small circular croutons
1 extra tablespoon butter for completion

Method

1. Gargir: Discard any yellowing leaves, wash and roughly chop, including parts of the stalk.
2. Cook the chopped onion in butter for 5 minutes.
3. Reduce the heat, throw in the roughly chopped gargir leaves and wilt in the butter and onion for no more than 5 minutes, turning occasionally.
4. Pour on the stock.
5. Throw in the shabat, kuzbara leaves, garlic, kuzbara seed, salt, and peppers.
6. Add the cooked potatoes.
7. Cover with 6 cups boiling water, add the beef cubes, and gently simmer for 6 minutes.
8. Blend the mixture for 6–8 seconds only, so that the gargir leaves do not become too broken up.
9. Make the croutons ahead of time and keep warm.
10. Ten minutes before serving, stir a small amount of the hot soup into the beaten yogurt. Once the yogurt is well mixed, stir all the yogurt into the soup.
11. Return to a bain-marie, add the extra butter and keep hot until ready to serve.

If the soup is kept hot too long, the delightful dark green color will turn brown. In this brownish state the soup is still excellent, but *Gargir* Soup is more alluring to the eye when it appears dark green. The finished consistency should be like that of a thin cream.

The soup can be served dark green, without yogurt, if preferred. Unlike some other soups *Gargir* Soup does not hold the heat for long, probably because it does not contain any thickening agent. Be sure, therefore, to make the soup really hot before serving, but not boiling, which will destroy the dark green color.

Serve in bowls with freshly made warm round croutons.

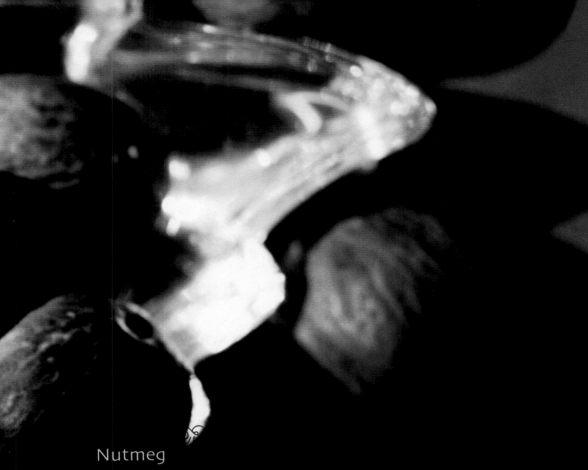

Nutmeg

The Banda Isles, remote in the Indian Ocean, are known as the Nutmeg Islands. When the nutmeg trees are in full bloom, the aroma of their flowers is so powerful that birds of paradise become intoxicated with their scent. Perhaps this is why they are birds of paradise.

Nutmeg, *Myristica fragrans*, such a beautiful Latin name, is mentioned by Sheikh al-Nafzawi (see page 12) as positively ravishing. It is, indeed, known to be one of the most powerful natural aphrodisiacs there is. Dr. Loutfy Boulos, in his *Medicinal Plants of North Africa*, says it is "dangerous even in moderate doses." But remember, even arsenic and antimony, in minute doses, are beneficial to man. Nutmeg is banned from Saudi Arabian supermarkets. Once, in Mexico, in an Acapulco store, I came across a whole counter piled high with little cans of ground nutmeg. But there must have been many disappointed 'flower children' in Acapulco. The nut, when whole, keeps its power for years, but when ground to a powder it quickly loses most of its mystical qualities. Hence the admonition in this recipe and others to grate the nutmeg into the soup at the last minute.

I have gathered the nuts from beneath shiny-leafed nutmeg trees in Kandy, Sri Lanka, and I have never noticed anything untoward in their use. Indeed, my family has been using nutmeg for generations, in curries, custards, and drinks. The tree provides two spices in one—the hard nut and the outer filigree covering known as 'mace.' Both spices impart wondrous fragrance, if not great 'feeling,' to our recipes, especially for Cream of *Sabanikh*.

Cream of *Sabanikh,* or Spinach Soup

A Soup of Delights—the stuff that dreams are made of

This Soup of Delights refers to delights of the mind as well as of the palate. It should be taken with lunch on a Sunday afternoon, or on a cold winter's night before retiring. If for lunch, couches-of-reverie should be provided for an afternoon nap. The soup does have certain psychedelic affinities with Alice B. Tokla's Hashish Fudge, sometimes causing gusts of laughter—but without any side effects.

Spinach and spinach-like leaves of various kinds are common in Egypt. One day, by chance, Mohamed, on making his usual spinach soup, added *kuzbara* (coriander) leaves and some *shabat* (dill), and the soup turned out to be not only a pleasant variation on spinach soup but seemed to give it a hint of Upper Egypt.

Ingredients for 6 servings

2 onions, thinly sliced into long strips

3 pearls garlic, put through a garlic press

2 cups chicken stock

1/2 kilogram fresh spinach (as you know, a mass of spinach cooks down to a very small amount)

2 cups kuzbara (coriander) leaves stripped from their stalks

1 cup water

1 cup shabat (dill) stripped from the stalk

2 cups roux (see page 26)

1/2 cup light cream

1/2 teaspoon white sugar

Salt, white pepper, and a large pinch (about 1/4 teaspoon) cayenne pepper

1 whole nutmeg, freshly grated into the soup at the last minute

Method

1. Partly cook the finely sliced onion and garlic in the chicken stock and set aside.
2. Place the washed spinach, coriander, and dill leaves in an earthenware or enamel pot with one cup of water.
3. Gently wilt for 5 minutes, no more, turning over and over.
4. It doesn't matter if the spinach is not quite cooked. Done this way it keeps the soup's dark green color.
5. Put the spinach and herbs through a moulinette, or, if you are very quick, use a blender for no more than 15 seconds. The spinach should not be broken up too much. Set aside.
6. Make 2 cupfuls of white roux, allowing to simmer and bubble gently for 10 minutes.
7. Slowly stir into the roux the onion, garlic, and chicken stock, and the hot spinach mixture.
8. Add cream, salt, white and cayenne pepper, and sugar.
9. Lastly, just before serving, grate and stir in one whole nutmeg.
10. Bring to a hot temperature again, but do not boil.
11. Serve with either crusty brown rolls or soft 'aysh baladi bread. Fingers of Welsh rarebit go well with this soup. If the soup is kept hot too long before serving, it will lose its lovely dark green color, but it will still taste the same.

Variation

At the flick of the wrist, Cream of *Sabanikh* can be turned into something akin to a delightful ancient Egyptian soup. Just before serving, prepare the following mixture:

1 cup Greek-style yogurt beaten to a smooth cream

1 teaspoon *kammun* (cumin)

1/2 cup slightly chopped *kuzbara* (coriander) leaves, in addition to those used in making the soup

Mix all together and add gradually to the main spinach soup, spoonful by spoonful, stirring all the time, so as not to curdle the yogurt. Bring to full heat, but not boiling, and serve immediately.

Ingredients for 4 servings

1 kilogram leeks
3 medium-sized onions
8 pearls of garlic, peeled and crushed just before using
6 black peppercorns
2 cups defatted beef stock or 3 beef bouillon cubes
3 bay leaves
1 teaspoon crushed or powdered thyme
2 cloves
Salt, freshly ground black pepper, and 1/4 teaspoon cayenne pepper
Yolk of 1 egg
1/2 cup light cream
1/2 glass white wine (optional)
A handful of chopped kuzbara (coriander) leaves or parsley

Roux mixture:
2 tablespoons unsalted butter
3 tablespoons flour
2 cups hot milk
2 cups hot meat stock

Croutons:
4 slices of white bread cut into rounds or small squares for croutons
3 tablespoons unsalted butter

Method

1. Clean and rinse the leeks thoroughly. Cut off the upper green part. Roughly chop the white stems into 5-cm (2-inch) pieces.
2. Peel and quarter the onions.
3. Cover leeks, onions, and garlic with water, add a few whole black peppercorns, and boil 10 minutes. Put through a moulinette, or blender, using all of the cooking liquid, and put aside.
4. Prepare a roux:
   Melt butter in a heavy enamel or iron pot. Once the butter is sizzling (do not let it burn), throw in the flour and stir vigorously with a wooden spoon until the butter has absorbed all the flour—a few seconds. Without delay, pour in a quarter of the hot milk and keep stirring briskly until the milk has melded with the butter-flour mixture. Pour in the remainder of the hot milk in stages and stir until absorbed into the roux.
5. Stir the meat stock into the roux. Reduce heat and let simmer gently for 10 minutes to allow the flour in the roux to cook.
6. Stir in the hot pureed mixture. Add the bay leaves, crushed thyme, and cloves, and let simmer for another 10 minutes. Add salt, freshly ground black pepper, and red cayenne pepper. Keep hot but do not let boil.
7. Make croutons:
   Cut the slices of white bread into 2.5-cm (1-inch) circles, or into small squares. Fry in butter until golden. Drain and keep warm.
8. Before serving, beat one egg yolk and optional wine into the cream. Very slowly, stir the egg/(wine)/cream mixture into the hot soup, stirring constantly until the soup thickens—about 5 minutes.
9. Simmer gently for another 5 minutes, using a bain-marie or a heat diffuser beneath the pot.
10. Just before serving, add a handful of finely chopped kuzbara (coriander) leaves, or parsley. Place 2–3 croutons in each soup bowl, pour hot soup over and serve.

Cream of Leek, Garlic, and Onion Soup

A tribute to the ancient Egyptians who cultivated onions, leeks, and garlic in profusion for thousands of years and used them as food as well as medicinally and religiously in their temple rituals.

Garlic

Both hated and loved, garlic *(Allium sativum)*, like onions and leeks, is a member of the renowned lily family—some lily! It is said that a garlic bulb planted under a rose bush helps to increase the fragrance of its flowers.

Garlic has been used in Egypt for at least four thousand years. Wandering in the wilderness during their long search to reach the Promised Land, the Israelites nostalgically remembered the "cucumbers, melons, leeks, onions, and garlic" they enjoyed in Egypt (Numbers, 11:5).

Until recently, before trucks took over, in late March and early April the tinkling bells of hundreds of horse and donkey carts could be heard in the streets as they brought mountains of the new season's garlic and onions to the walls of al-Hakim's eleventh-century mosque—the traditional place in Cairo for bulk sales. To see these 'mountains' of garlic is to remember the ancient papyrus texts that refer to the knotting of bunches of onions and garlic as a tiring task. The knotting is still necessary to send the plant's strength down into the bulb.

The centuries-old site in Cairo for marketing the new season's bulk sales of garlic and onions was, until recently, outside the walls of al-Hakim's eleventh-century mosque and commonly known as Suq al-Lamun, even though lemons were rarely sold there.

Onions

As with garlic, the ancient Egyptians attributed religious and healing powers to the onion. On the arrival of the new season's crop, special festivals were held. Paintings in tombs and reliefs on temple walls at Sakkara, Memphis, and Thebes, made over three thousand years ago, show priests holding up bunches of onions. Other reliefs show bunches of onions tied in knots hung around the throat and stomach of temple priests. There were also special days 'for chewing onions.'

The ancient cult of the onion continues in Egypt, and onions are used today in vast quantities. Don't be afraid at the thought of using so much garlic and so many leeks and onions in one soup. Just thank God for one of His greatest gifts to mankind, and enjoy it.

Cream of Lentil Soup

A variation on the traditional Egyptian lentil soup

Lentils are as old as Egypt. So are cumin, onions, and garlic, the three essential ingredients for this soup.

In winter the Sa'idis, the Upper Egyptians, traditionally begin their day with *shurbat 'ads*, a lentil soup, as others might start their day with a plate of hot porridge. This is my own version of what is an ancient Egyptian soup.

Shay bi-l-Na'na'—Mint Tea

After a large bowl of lentil soup, most Egyptians love a glass of mint tea. This is made by putting the leaves and stalk of the na'na' (fresh mint) into the teapot to steep, along with the tea, for a few minutes. Serve in small tea glasses, without milk, but sugar if you wish, and an extra sprig of fresh mint in each tea glass.

Ingredients for 6 servings

3–4 cups yellow lentils
Enough meat or chicken stock, or water, to cover
2 bay leaves
6 medium-sized onions, thinly sliced lengthwise
4 cups milk
8 pearls garlic, thinly sliced
2 finely diced and cooked carrots
1 tablespoon cumin
1/2 cup light cream
1 tablespoon white sugar
1/2 cup red wine (optional)
1/2 cup lime or lemon juice
Salt, freshly ground black pepper, and red cayenne
    pepper
Handful of parsley, finely chopped
Freshly made warm croutons

Method

1. Wash the lentils thoroughly in cold water and remove any small stones or stalks.
2. Cover with water or stock.
3. Add bay leaves and salt, and simmer until almost cooked.
4. Stir occasionally, otherwise the lentils have a tendency to stick to the bottom of the pot and to burn quickly.
5. Puree the lentils either in a blender, or through a moulinette—if necessary, dilute with a little more water or stock. Set aside.
6. Cook the finely sliced onions in water for 5 minutes.
7. Pour on the milk and bring to a gentle simmer for another 5 minutes.
8. Add the cooked onion and hot milk to the pureed lentils, diluting if necessary to a preferred soup consistency.
9. Add sugar, freshly ground black pepper, red cayenne pepper, thinly sliced garlic, and diced carrot.
10. Simmer in a bain-marie or double boiler for 5 minutes and keep hot.
11. Just before serving stir in the lemon or lime juice, add the half-cup of light cream and the optional red wine, and the parsley.
12. Keep hot in the bain-marie of boiling water until ready to serve.
13. Serve with either 'aysh baladi, toasted 'aysh shami, or, best of all, freshly made warm croutons.

Potage de la Monastère

Herb Soup
Ambrosial

Far be it from me to blow my own trumpet, but I can only repeat what Prince Hassan Aziz Hassan said at dinner one night: "This is one of the great soups of the world." And he should know, having in his day dined in the restaurants of Paris and Geneva.

The recipe for this soup began many years ago, in faraway New Zealand, as my Spanish Soup—basically tomato, onion, sherry, and cream. Over the years it went on evolving in Canada, still as a Spanish Soup, and reached its peak of perfection years later in Egypt under the name of Potage de la Monastère because of all the herbs used from a monastery herb garden. It is still basically a tomato soup.

There was a time, not so long ago, when the tomato was known in Egypt as 'the funny fruit' (and you could call this soup the Funny Fini Soup, but that would never do). The whim of the season, such as a slight drop in temperature during the night, could cause violent fluctuations in the daily market price of the tomatoes in Cairo. In those days tomatoes were ridiculously cheap—usually no more than a few piasters a kilogram. But if a cold night hit the Delta region the price could soar, overnight, to 20 piasters, which was still very little money. And what wonderful sun-ripened tomatoes they were.

Alas, gone are the days of 5–20 piaster tomatoes. Indeed, almost gone are the full-flavored, sun-ripened tomatoes themselves we used to know as *baladi* or 'ace' tomatoes. In their place we now have a supposedly improved new tomato, dreamed up by a visiting Danish horticulturalist, their long shelf-life assured. Now and again, if you search diligently, you can still find the old 'funny' tomatoes in lowly souks, but never in supermarkets.

To make this soup successfully, you must use soft, red, sun-ripened fruit and not hard, tasteless tomatoes that have been kissing cellophane in a supermarket for a week. It is a waste of time trying to make this delicious soup with the new kind of pink or hard red tomatoes,

The Herbs
The good things of Egypt

Kuzbara, Coriander (or Cilantro), *Coriandrum sativum*

Kuzbara, coriander, was one of the bitter herbs used when the Israelites were preparing to leave Egypt. Pliny thought that the best coriander came from Egypt, where it was mixed with wine and used for heart and liver troubles. Dr. Loutfy Boulos, in his *Medicinal Plants of North Africa*, will tell you that when taken in large enough quantities, coriander is an aphrodisiac. It is one of the key ingredients Scheherazade gives in her love potions in the story of Alaa al-Din (Aladdin), of *One Thousand and One Nights* fame. An old English proverb confirms that the potency of coriander has the power to induce love, "if gathered in the last quarter of the moon."

I once brought back to Cairo a few *kuzbara* seeds given to me by a friend in Montreal. Though I thought this was a bit like bringing 'coals to Newcastle,' Mohamed diligently planted the Canadian seeds in a pot, which he kept on the kitchen windowsill. Nothing happened, until one day I noticed a few specks of green emerging from the soil. I excitedly called Mohamed who explained: "Yes, the Canadian *kuzbara* was sleeping, so I planted some Egyptian."

Shabat, Dill, *Anethum graveolens*

Dill has always grown wild around the shores of the Mediterranean. The word in English means 'to lull.' Especially loved and widely used by Poles, Ukrainians, and Russians, in Egypt we use masses of dill, especially in this original recipe for Potage de la Monastère.

Ba'dunis, Parsley, *Petroselinum crispum*

What a ghastly Latin name for delightful parsley, which is used as an appetizer and a stimulant. Like Egyptian *gargir*, it is oozing with iron.

Tarragon, *Artemesia dranunculus*

Whoever dreamt up such a Latin name for this most mystical of herbs? Tarragon came originally from somewhere in Central Asia. It is rarely grown in Egypt so we rely on imported, dried tarragon. It is a most essential herb for the soup.

Toum, Garlic, *Allium sativum*

According to Herodotus, on a stone in the Great Pyramid of Cheops, built around 2600 BC, there was an inscription in hieroglyphs recording the daily quantity of radishes, onions, and garlic consumed by the men working on the largest structure ever built by man. Another text refers to the workers engaged on building the pyramid as going on strike because they were not being given their daily ration of garlic. It has long been a wonder herb of Egyptian culinary, religious, and medicinal fame. It was one of the main ingredients of Roman love potions, a wickedly effective aphrodisiac, and valued by Greek athletes training for their feats of strength and agility at Olympia.

Basal, Onions, *Allium cepa*

Some think the onion first appeared in Siberia. Others say Asia. Though what causes plants to appear in one place rather than another only God knows, and he's not telling.

Ingredients for 6 servings

1 kilogram sun-ripened tomatoes, or, if you dare, 5 cups of good quality tomato juice

2 medium-sized onions, halved and finely sliced lengthwise

3 bay leaves

Masses of fresh herbs, prepared in advance:

3 cups fresh shabat (dill), stripped from its stalks and finely cut

2 cups fresh kuzbara (coriander) leaves, stripped from their stalks and roughly chopped—kuzbara is at its best not cut too much; it then imparts its flavor in the mouth, rather than dissipating its flavor in the soup

2 cups ba'dunis (parsley), finely cut

3 tablespoons dried tarragon, or 1 cup fresh tarragon, stripped from the stalk and finely chopped

4–5 pearls garlic, finely chopped

1 tablespoon white sugar

Small amount of salt, freshly ground white pepper

1/4 teaspoon red pepper

1/2 cup dry sherry, or gin (optional)

Juice of 6 big green limes

1 cup whipped cream sweetened with a teaspoon of sugar

Method

1. Cover the tomatoes with boiling water, leave for two minutes, cool and de-skin. Put the tomatoes through a moulinette. A blender can be used, but the moulinette doesn't break up the tomato so much. Keep aside.
2. Cook the onions in half the tomato juice until almost, but not quite, cooked, about 10 minutes.
3. Add the chopped garlic
4. Stir in the rest of the tomato pulp, or juice.
5. Add bay leaves, sugar, and dried tarragon (or finely chopped fresh tarragon). Dried tarragon can be rubbed in the fingers almost to a powder. Add salt, pepper, and red pepper.
6. Bring the soup to a simmer for 10 minutes.
7. Ten minutes before serving, stir in all the prepared herbs—shabat, ba'dunis, and kuzbara—followed by the optional sherry or gin, and the fresh lime juice.

In its finished state, the soup should not go on cooking too much, to ensure the onion is still slightly under-cooked, the tomato juice is still fresh, rather than cooked, and the herbs remain green. Float a very large spoonful of whipped and sweetened cream on the surface of each bowl of soup. Serve with crisp 'aysh shami, or thin Melba toast.

Cream of Lettuce Soup

A Soup for Shamm al-Nasim

If not aphrodisiac, 'dream-like'

To make this soup—a tribute to the pharaohs of ancient Egypt who knew a thing or two about lettuce—you will need either an electric blender or a moulinette.

Khass in Arabic, *laitue* in French, lettuce, should you not know, is the Herb of Dreams. The Arabic name *khass* probably comes from the Greek *cos*, and either the long Egyptian lettuce (*khass baladi*) or iceberg lettuce can be used in this recipe. Whichever lettuce you use, be sure to use only the outer dark green leaves, for their flavor.

When I was eight years old, I wanted a garden, because children love to grow things. Among my plants were a few lettuce seedlings my mother contributed. While cutting one of my lettuces for lunch one day, I noticed a white liquid, like milk, oozing from the cut stalks. That's funny, I thought, milk coming out of lettuce? Little did I know, and few know today, that this white milk is the stuff that dreams are made of. Indeed, there is more to a single lettuce leaf than first meets the eye.

The ancient Egyptians knew why. And the Greeks, who probably got it from the Egyptians, regarded lettuce as having a calming effect.

Pictures engraved on the walls of Egyptian tombs show Pharaoh offering piles of lettuce, a meter high, to the god Min, god of fertility. And, sometimes, dare I relate, wall pictures show Pharaoh standing by a pile of the tall Egyptian lettuce plants with his penis fully extended. But the ancients don't say just how much to eat.

There is an old French provincial custom, used to this day, to induce sleep in little ones reluctant to go to sleep. Given a small piece of white lettuce stalk to suck, no more than a few centimeters long, the little one will nod off into dreamland in no time at all. But do French mothers know what the ancient Egyptians knew all along? The white milk-like juice I found oozing out of my garden lettuce contains, of all things, a substance similar to that found in the milk of the evil opium poppy, though presumably not in such a concentrated

form. Having banned powerful erotic nutmegs from Saudi grocery shelves, goodness knows what the religious police of al-Khobar will do once they find out about fresh garden lettuce.

Besides its dream-inducing qualities, lettuce is also a powerful antibiotic. And recent research has shown it has a destructive effect on fatty particles in the blood, known to us as wicked cholesterol. But then not all cholesterol is bad; some is positively good and necessary. Formulas given in medicinal pharmacopoeias spell out the exact amount of 'tincture of oil' obtained from lettuce seeds necessary to counter impotence. Not that we dabble with lettuce seed oil in our recipe—only the fresh green leaves. However, be all this as it may, I notice that not all kinds of today's lettuce produce the precious white milk. And the kind of lettuce the ancients used does not look exactly like the iceberg kind.

Today, Egypt hasn't entirely forgotten all of its ancient herbal wisdom. On the feast of Shamm al-Nasim, the only pharaonic feast still celebrated in Egypt, by both Christians and Muslims, the streets are full of hand-pushed carts piled high with mountains of fresh lettuce, which on this festive day we are urged to eat in abundance.

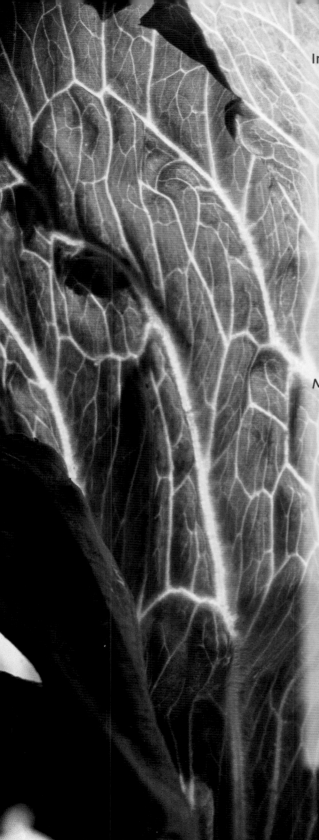

Ingredients for 4 servings

1 cup roughly chopped onion or scallions

2–3 pearls garlic, peeled and roughly chopped

7 cups washed and shredded outer (dark green) lettuce leaves

1 cup chopped shabat (dill)

2 tablespoons chopped parsley leaves

4 cups hot chicken or vegetable stock

1 tablespoon dried tarragon leaves or 2 tablespoons chopped fresh tarragon

1 tablespoon ground kuzbara (coriander) seed

2 tablespoons unsalted butter

2 tablespoons white flour

1 cup light cream

3/4 teaspoon salt

1/4 teaspoon freshly ground white pepper

1/4 teaspoon red cayenne pepper

1 teaspoon white sugar

Method

1. Melt butter in a large, heavy saucepan and cook chopped onion and garlic for 4 minutes, stirring occasionally.
2. Stir in 4 cups of the shredded lettuce, and the shabat, kuzbara seed, chopped parsley, and tarragon leaves. Cook and wilt for 2 minutes only, stirring occasionally. Then add remaining 3 cups of lettuce and cook for 2 more minutes. This tends to keep the soup greener.
3. Sprinkle in flour, stir well, and cook for 2 more minutes.
4. Pour in hot chicken or vegetable stock gradually, stir well, and simmer for 7 minutes.
5. Blend the mixture for 15 seconds only.
6. Return to the pot and bring to a simmer.
7. Pour in cream and season with salt, peppers, and sugar.

Serve with croutons of fried bread in butter, or with 'aysh shami, or, best of all, warm cheese straws.

Terfas, Truffles, *Terfezia genera*

Like all truffles, the desert truffle of Egypt is born mysteriously, out of sight, in darkness, just below the surface of the sand. The Bedouin of the desert say thunder and lightning are needed for their mystical creation. After an initial clap of thunder and a flash of lightning, followed by heavy rains in late autumn, the spores start germinating.

But even if the rains come at the right time, the weather must remain dry during January, otherwise late rain rots the truffles. Drat the thought.

Like all truffles, desert truffles have quite a 'reputation.' There is an ancient Roman saying that "those who wish to lead virtuous lives should abstain from truffles" and that "they render women more tender and men more loving." Even in pharaonic times, ancient papyrus writings of four thousand years ago tell us these strange desert fungi were served to Pharaoh with their mystical powers clearly in mind. The tables of the Fatimid caliphs of Cairo were also graced with truffles gathered from the nearby Muqattam Hills, and in the nineteenth century truffles were sold in such quantities in Cairo's souks "that far from being choice dainties, they were cheap and common" (Stanley Lane-Poole, *A History of Egypt*, Volume VI, 1901).

Alas, today, hardly anyone in Egypt has ever heard of them. Yet they do exist—in abundance. But 'progress' has swept them from the Muqattam Hills, and you must search for them far away in the Western Desert, close to the Egyptian–Libyan border. Wrinkled and gnarled when dug up, and slightly perfumed, desert truffles look like bruised potatoes, wizened walnuts, or dried prunes.

But their appearance is deceptive, and part of their mystique. Brown, black, creamy white, sometimes pink—should a basket of desert truffles ever come your way, you need to know what to do with them. Here is my trusted and tried original recipe for Créme de Truffe du Désert, always tasting better in French.

Truffles—if only you can find them. From Morocco to the Arabian Peninsula, their surface signs are subtle at best. A careful eye can spot the hint of a hump in the sand, or the symbiont grasses. Then, move quickly. Exposed to light and air, desert truffles pass their peak in about four days.

Ingredients for 4 servings

9 or 10 medium-sized white desert truffles, very fresh

4 cups whole milk or light cream

1 small onion, peeled and roughly chopped

2 or 3 pearls garlic, peeled and roughly chopped

4 more cups whole milk or light cream

1 tablespoon unsalted butter

2 tablespoons white all-purpose flour

1 beef bouillon cube

1/2 tablespoon granulated sugar

Salt and freshly ground white pepper

1/4 teaspoon cayenne pepper

3/4 cup light cream

1 teaspoon unsalted butter

Method

1. Immerse the truffles in cold water for 10 minutes. Throw out the water and loose sand and cover them with water again. Repeat.

2. Gently massage each truffle under running water with your fingers, then scrub them gently with a vegetable or mushroom brush and rinse. Scrub and rinse again. Some will tell you never to peel a truffle and to take out the remaining specks of sand with a fine-pointed knife. Nonsense! Much of the sand is invisible, so there is only one way to get rid of it.

3. Peel the truffles very finely—but don't throw away the peelings; they are very rich in flavor and add a deft light-brown tinge to the soup.

4. Barely cover the peelings with milk (amount not included in ingredients above) and simmer for 10 minutes. Let them stand so that the remaining fine sand sinks to the bottom. Cool.

5. Gently pour off the milk, leaving the sand behind, and reserve the milk. Discard the peelings.

6. Roughly chop all but two of the peeled truffles. Put the onion and garlic in the first 4 cups of milk and bring it to a boil. Boil for 5 minutes, then add the chopped truffles. Simmer gently for another 3 minutes, no longer. Purée mixture in a blender or a moulinette, and set it aside.

7. Make a white roux:
Use a heavy-bottomed saucepan and a heat diffuser between pot and burner. Heat the remaining 4 cups of milk to very hot (but do not boil) and hold it at this temperature. Melt 1 tablespoon of the butter; when it starts to froth, turn down the heat, stir in the flour and keep stirring until the butter absorbs all the flour and becomes a thick paste. Without delay, pour in the very hot milk, 1/2 cup at a time. Keep stirring without pausing until a smooth, creamy, thick sauce is achieved. If there are lumps, keep stirring until the bubbling sauce is smooth. Let it simmer very gently for another 10 minutes.

8. Slowly stir in the puréed truffle mixture until it is absorbed into the sauce. Drop in the bouillon cube and the sugar. Add salt, and white and cayenne pepper.

9. Gently, so as not to lift any remaining sand from the bottom, stir in the milk the peelings were boiled in. Stir in the 3/4 cup of cream and the butter for finishing. If the soup seems too thick, dilute with a little more milk.

10. At the very last minute before serving, to obtain the maximum truffle flavor, take the two peeled truffles you have set aside and grate them, using a rasp or the finest part of a kitchen grater, directly into the soup. Keep the soup hot, with the lid on, in a double boiler, and do not let it boil again.

Stored in a sealed jar in the refrigerator, the finished soup will keep its truffle flavor for several days.

Crème de Truffe du Désert

Aphrodisiac

For this recipe you'll need not only a basket of white desert truffles but also a female camel. If a camel isn't handy, you can use cow's milk or, even better, light cream.

If the truffles are fresh, the soup should possess a delicate truffle flavor and a most luxurious texture. If you have been lucky enough to find one or two truffles with a pink interior, it will have a seductive pink tinge. It is especially good served with warm cheese-straw pastries.

Cold
Soups

The flowering of apricot trees throughout the Nile Delta, in February, is the first sign of the Egyptian spring, bringing with it the promise of a luscious bounty to come.

Iced Soups

Iced vegetable and fruit soups of summer are culinary delights in many lands—Spanish *gazpacho*, made with cucumber and tomato and many herbs, Polish iced pink-beet *chlodnik* (meaning 'cool') soup; Turkish *cacik* using more cooling cucumbers, mint, and yogurt; Austrian cherry and iced plum soups; the Greek *tarata;* the Russian *okroschka* soup, using cucumber and sorrel; cold 'beer' soup from Ukraine; and the iced watercress soup of England. Apart from iced consommé, iced soups don't seem to belong much in France. *Vichyssoise*, iced potato and leek soup, despite its French name, and its creation by a French chef, is classed as 'American,' because that was where it was created, although it is firmly based on traditional French potato and leek soup.

In a hot and dusty land like Egypt, iced summer soups can be ambrosial—'food sent by the gods.' It is almost worthwhile putting up with the humidity of July and August in Egypt so as to be able to enjoy an iced summer potage. Such iced delights can be enjoyed in temperate lands too, but it should really be a very hot day to relish and desire them. Hot weather is one of the ingredients.

In centuries past, Egypt had no 'ice' to play with. But they got around this in the twelfth and fourteenth centuries by bringing snow all the way to Cairo from the mountains of Lebanon, organizing daily camel 'ice' caravans, and, later, in specially built 'ice ships,' manned by 'snowmen' trained to get the ice to Cairo as quickly as possible. The delights of the snow merchant's trade entered the realms of poetry and Scheherazade's *One Thousand and One Nights*.

The temperature of iced soups: Just as a hot soup must be served piping hot, and within minutes can become lukewarm, so too, iced soups must be served very, very cold. Within minutes they can melt, especially in Egypt, and become a disappointment. Just 'cold' for an iced soup equates with a 'lukewarm' hot soup. Serving iced soups in summer, temperature control is vital.

Note carefully: In Egypt we are singularly blessed by being able to find luscious sun-ripened ingredients. To make these iced soups successfully, you need *sun-ripened* strawberries, apricots, full-red pomegranates, not pale ones, and sun-ripened tomatoes. You will not have much success if you use the supermarket varieties that have usually been picked half-ripe and left to 'ripen' by devious means to ensure their long shelf-life.

Iced Apricot Soup

Made with a touch of arsenic, and a small hammer
Ambrosial

The people of Hunza who live in the high Karakoram Mountains between China and Pakistan, are noted for their long life-expectancy, living to an average age of 90–100 years. Their basic diet is a simple one of corn, barley, lentils, buttermilk, unleavened bread, goat's meat, cheese, new wine, tea—and a passion for consuming masses of apricots. In summer they devour them fresh off the trees. During winter they use them dried in their cooking. And despite what the French peasants have long said about the kernels of apricots—that eating them causes madness—the people of Hunza grind them into a flour, and press them to produce their cooking oil. They also traditionally fatten little Hunza babies on a teaspoon of apricot oil a day. So perhaps a little arsenic, contained in the apricot kernel, does you good. Otherwise, how do the people of Hunza get away with it? Living high up in the Karakoram mountains they do, of course, enjoy pure mountain air and drink only crystal clear snow-water—in a kind of Shangri-La environment.

Here, at last, is the secret recipe for Feeney's Iced Apricot Soup, for years sought after by visitors from Dhahran, Paris, and London. It must be the only soup in the world requiring the use of a small hammer and a touch of arsenic. Like many of the good things to eat, it is very simple to make and exudes the full flavor of apricots—'ambrosial,' in our terms. So, get busy with your hammer, forget what French peasants say about the kernels, and put your faith in the Himalayan people of Hunza. Along with their apricots, and a touch of arsenic, many of them live to a hundred years. *Take* one kilogram of sun-ripened apricots . . .

46

Ingredients for 4 servings

1 kilogram ripe, halved, and pitted apricots; never, never dried or canned apricots, which won't work in this recipe

A 10-cm (4-inch) piece of peeled and roughly chopped fresh root ginger; if the ginger root is
very young and tender, it can be scraped, rather than peeled

3 strips finely peeled orange rind

1 teaspoon powdered ginger

2–3 tablespoons white sugar, depending on the sweetness of the apricots

Juice of 6 oranges, plus the juice of 2 more oranges for finishing; Egyptian 'summer' (sweet) oranges are best

3 cups Greek- or Turkish-style yogurt

Kernels of 9 dried apricot stones, peeled and roughly chopped, or, instead, two drops—exactly, and no more—of almond essence; measure the drops out very carefully: too much completely overpowers the apricot flavor

The use of one small hammer:

To extract the kernels, place each stone, separately, in a folded tea-towel, holding the stone in place with the fingers on top of the towel, and using the hammer in the other hand. Hit each stone gently so as not to completely smash the shell. Just the right hit will break the shell and release a whole kernel. Peel the thin brown skin off the whole kernel.

This is where 'a touch of arsenic' comes in. We know that apricot kernels contain arsenic—so the French peasants are not altogether wrong about madness. But, on the other hand, the people of Hunza, bless them, thrive on it.

Method

1. Put orange juice, peeled and powdered ginger, kernels, and sugar into a blender and blend at liquidizer speed for about 20 seconds.
2. Add the halved, de-stoned apricots and 1 cup of water and blend for another 15 seconds, no more. If the blender's holder is too small for all the apricots, blend in two operations and then mix together.
3. Add yogurt and blend for another 10 seconds.

If an electric blender is not available, the same procedure can be followed using a moulinette, in which case the ginger should be grated finely and the kernels fine-chopped before grinding in the moulinette, along with the apricots, yogurt, and orange juice.

If the soup is too thick, dilute with a little more orange juice. If it is too tart, add another spoonful of sugar. Pour the soup into a thin container and place in the freezing compartment of the refrigerator for about 20–30 minutes, depending on the power of the refrigerator. Just before serving, stir in the additional orange juice. The soup should be served on a summer's day, very, very cold, just as it is starting to ice. Serve with thin wafers of crisp Melba toast or crisp 'aysh shami, or, best of all, freshly warmed cheese straws.

Iced Strawberry Soup

Ambrosial and Aphrodisiac

On more than one occasion it has been noted that partaking of this Iced Strawberry Soup provides a relaxed sensation and a general sense of well-being for several hours afterwards.

It has even been known to arouse in some people a slight sense of joviality, a 'happiness with life.' But then the very idea of the strawberry, a distant cousin of the rose and the cape gooseberry, as an 'iced soup,' is enough to arouse joviality in anyone with a fine sense of humor.

It may at first seem a strange soup to serve. In Egypt it's a soup of springtime, when local strawberries are at their best. The ripest usually arrive on the streets about midday, gathered by farmer's wives in the morning and sold from huge straw baskets, carefully weighed out on small hand-held scales.

Elsewhere, it may be possible to get sun-ripened strawberries at any time of the year, but be sure they *are* sun-ripened—otherwise the recipe can be a disaster. Generally speaking, beware of strawberries sold in tightly covered plastic containers, which have usually been picked green and ripened by devious means other than the sun.

Serving note: For some reason, perhaps because it is so ravishing, Iced Strawberry Soup is almost a meal in itself. Once supped, anything else seems superfluous. It is best to treat it this way. Prince Hassan suggested the only thing to go with this soup, along with the toasted almonds, is champagne, or another sparkling wine. I heartily agree.

Ingredients for 4 servings

The nubs of six young shoots (tender sprouts) of fresh ginger—otherwise, scrape and clean a 4-cm (1.5-inch) piece of root-ginger and roughly chop

2 tablespoons white sugar—depending on the sweetness of the strawberries

Juice of 2 sweet oranges

5 cups, or about 1 kilogram, firm sun-ripened strawberries—not in any way mushy—select them carefully

2 cups Greek- or Turkish-style yogurt

2 teaspoons freshly grated nutmeg—never powdered, which has lost its efficacy

Juice of half a lime, or a quarter of a lemon

Small bowl of freshly roasted almonds

Method

1. Put chopped ginger, sugar, and orange juice into blender and liquidize in about 20 seconds

2. Add the strawberries and blend for another 10 seconds

3. Add the yogurt, nutmeg, and lime (or lemon) juice, and blend for another 10 seconds.

4. Pour into a thin-sided container and place in the freezing compartment of refrigerator for about 30 minutes, until icy. Remove, beat, and stir to a soup consistency and serve immediately, very cold and icy, preferably in chilled glass bowls, with thin Melba toast and a bowl of freshly roasted almonds.

Delice Persan Froid
Iced Pomegranate Soup
Ambrosial and Aphrodisiac

I wouldn't say this soup puts me in a class with Alice B. Tokla, God rest her soul, and her recipe for Hashish Fudge. No "Food of Paradise," no "euphoria or storms of laughter," as Alice would say. Though goodness knows, a pink soup is enough to make anyone scream with hilarity. Some believe the soup is one of my most exquisite concoctions. It is one of our Egyptian discoveries, and though conceived in Egypt it can be made anywhere that good pomegranates are to be found in season. But they must be fresh, with their bloom still upon them, not dry and shriveled like many supermarket specimens. To this moment I have not seen or heard of anyone else making this kind of soup. In spite of its name, it has nothing to do with Persia, other than that Persia produces probably the best pomegranate juice in the world, and the fact that the color of the soup is a pure Persian pink.

Intuitively, I had always thought pomegranates, the fruit of the goddess Aphrodite, must surely be aphrodisiac and of course, as it turns out, they are. In Cyprus the fruit is looked upon as a fertility symbol. Certainly in our Delice Persan, when the juice is combined with *freshly grated* nutmeg (and you know what Sheikh al-Nafzawi, in his little volume "The Perfumed Garden," has to say about nutmeg), the aphrodisiac power of the soup is truly enhanced. But in what measure, who can say? Except the Sheikh!

Besides Persia, I have also had very good pomegranate juice in Samarkand and in southern Spain. The soup was named by Prince Hassan, who came to lunch on 3 September 1977, and apart from myself was the first to taste Delice Persan. Or, in plain English, Iced Pomegranate Soup. Delice Persan Froid should not be confused with Delice Persan Chaud, which is an entirely different hot soup. Hassan said it should really be called Turkish Delight. But as you know, there is already a Turkish Delight, a delicacy of another kind. So I suggested Persian Delight, and we settled for Delice Persan, mainly because of the soup's lovely soft pink color. Otherwise, it might well have become, dare I say it, Fini's Persian Pink.

Like most of our original summer fruit soup recipes, this one is very simple to make. But note that pomegranate juice, when freshly squeezed, is an extremely powerful liquid. Never let it come into contact with metal. Always use glass, enamel, or earthenware containers. The quality of the soup can vary with the acidity of the pomegranates used. The richest, sweetest pomegranate juice makes for a more delectable potage

Hints on serving Iced Pomegranate Soup

To serve a fresh iced pink soup is a most unusual situation to have on your hands and you should make the most of it. If possible, use two glass bowls, one inside the other. Pack the outer bowl with crushed ice and use the inner bowl to hold the delicate pink soup. For an even more dramatic effect, use a silver bowl in which to hold the soup, inside a larger glass bowl packed with ice. The silver and pink make for a most ecstatic effect. (A silver-*plated* bowl will not be affected by the powerful pomegranate juice, by this stage well diluted with other ingredients.)

An hour or so after ingesting Delice Persan Froid, a general sense of well-being may become apparent. The use of an adequate amount of *freshly* grated nutmeg added to the soup, at the very last stage of preparation, should induce sound sleep and even pleasant dreams during an afternoon siesta. If, by chance, a subliminal state is not immediately achieved, don't be discouraged—try some more soup. Now, all you need are 2 kilograms of ripe pomegranates, a hot summer day, . . .

Ingredients for 4 servings

    5 cups of already prepared pomegranate juice extracted from about 2 kilograms of ripe fruit; the way of extracting the juice is explained on page 16

    3 cups yogurt beaten to a very smooth cream

    1–2 tablespoons, more or less, depending on the acidity of the fruit, of white sugar

    Juice of 2–3 small green limes (not aged yellow ones)

    2 teaspoons fresh root ginger, peeled and roughly chopped

    1 tablespoon freshly grated nutmeg—finely grated on a nutmeg grater; never use powdered nutmeg

    A small grinding of fresh white pepper

    1 extra teaspoon freshly grated nutmeg for finishing

    Pinch of salt

A certain amount of adjustment is always needed depending on the sweetness of the fruit, but there must never be too much sugar or lime juice.

Method

1. Place the loose seeds in a blender (or a moulinette).
2. Turn at liquidizing speed for 20 seconds.
3. Strain off the juice into a glass or enamel container. Return the seed residue remaining in the strainer back into the blender. Pour on one cup of cold water and blend again for a few seconds. Pour back into the strainer and press hard with a wooden spoon, extracting the rich remaining residue, which can greatly enhance the texture and flavor of the soup.
4. Use one cup of juice in which to 'blend' the chopped ginger and add to the juice.
5. Stir in the creamed yogurt, followed by the lime juice, white pepper, freshly grated nutmeg, and pinch of salt.
6. Thoroughly chill in the freezing compartment of the refrigerator until just beginning to make flaky ice. Keep the iced soup in this state until ready to serve. If the soup goes past the flaky ice stage and becomes too icy—or even solid ice—tip out and crush either with an electric beater or a potato masher and then whip into the flaky ice stage again. Lastly, just before serving add the extra teaspoon of freshly grated nutmeg. Be sure to serve with very thin crisp 'aysh shami or Melba toast.

Iced Guava Soup

Take one to two kilograms (depending on size) of ripe but firm guavas, and a few oranges and limes.

One guava can perfume a room, which is not surprising, for the guava is related to the cinnamon tree of Sri Lanka, the clove of Zanzibar, and the eucalyptus tree of Australia. So what wouldn't be perfumed after dipping into these three exotics? The guava's flesh can be either creamy white or rose pink set around a mass of very hard inedible seeds. In our Heliopolis garden we are blessed by a tree producing small but well flavored fruit and which we call Linda's Tree. If you are fortunate enough to come across rare pink guavas, you are halfway to Paradise. Unlike the vibrant pink of Pomegranate Soup, pink guavas make for a most delicate pale pink soup of almost celestial translucency.

Ingredients for 6 servings

- 10 to 20 medium-sized firm, not soft, guavas
- 1 tablespoon freshly peeled and chopped ginger
- Juice of 8 medium-sized green limes
- Juice of 2 'sugar' oranges
- 2 tablespoons white sugar
- 1 tablespoon dried mint
- 1 cup water
- 2 cups milk
- Half a cup of gin (optional)
- Juice of 1 orange for completion
- Juice of 1 lime for completion
- 1 cup Greek- or Turkish-style yogurt, beaten to a creamy consistency

Method

To make the base:

1. Wash and peel the guavas, keeping the skins.
2. Slice off the flesh from the seed-cores and sprinkle with a little lime juice to prevent discoloring.
3. Place seeds and skin in a bowl and barely cover with water (about 2 cups). Leave for three hours. Strain and reserve.
4. Put chopped ginger, lime juice, orange juice, sugar, and mint into a blender with one cup of water and liquidize for about 15 seconds.
5. Put guava flesh, milk, and the strained water from the seeds and skin into the same blended mixture and blend 5 more seconds. Add the optional gin.
6. Store this base for the soup in glass jars in refrigerator.

Completion:

1. To the base mixture add the additional orange and lime juice.
2. Stir in the creamed yogurt.
3. Chill to just freezing stage, or until ice is beginning to form.
4. Serve immediately in Chinese bowls, with Chinese porcelain spoons and either crisp 'aysh shami or Melba toast.

Iced Melon Soup

Ambrosial

This can be a most ravishing iced soup. But its ambrosial quality depends in large measure upon using a sun-ripened melon. Salmon-colored and white-fleshed melons, like those from Ismailiya in Egypt, are good, but best of all are the pale green-fleshed galia melons from Sinai. A similar melon from Spain can sometimes be found, and makes an excellent substitute.

A ripe melon usually exudes a soft scent and is said to be ripe when its surface, scraped with a fingernail, reveals a green skin beneath. The seating of the stem should also be slightly sunken.

A Street of Melons, in Samarkand. For a man seated upon a quilted mat with a pot of green Uzbek tea and a basket of grapes nearby, the morning passes peacefully.

Melons in Excelsis

Who could have imagined that the succulent melon, scented with musk and honey-flavored, palest pink, yellow, or jade green, is descended from the lowly pumpkin and marrow family, and related to the cucumber? Melons are as old as Egypt. The Israelites wandering in the wilderness longed for Egyptian melons. Various kinds are found growing wild all over Africa, and they have been cultivated in Egypt since the days of antiquity—melon seeds are sometimes found among funerary offering in the tombs of the ancients.

According to Egyptian tradition, a melon should be cut an hour or so before a meal and left to cool in the air. The evaporation of the juice on the cut surface cools the melon—in the same way as a sweating Egyptian clay water-pot cools the water inside. In these days of refrigeration, cutting the melon early doesn't really matter. Another piece of ancient advice is that once it is cut it is always wise to watch the melon, lest a serpent come and poison the fruit with its bite: reptiles are extremely fond of melons and can smell their aroma from a great distance.

All this having been said, the recipe for Iced Melon Soup is not Egyptian, but the melons used always are. The recipe comes from China, where they have long treasured melons as containing 'the nectar of Paradise.'

Melons are grown in profusion in the salty, sandy wastes surrounding the oasis of Samarkand. Watered by the melting snows of the nearby Celestial Mountains, for centuries Samarkand's melons were sent by camel caravan to the imperial court in Peking, in lead containers packed with ice.

I first tasted Iced Melon Soup, by chance, for lunch one day in Hong Kong. The melon had come by air from the province of Sinkiang, in Chinese Central Asia, not far from Samarkand. The soup was sheer bliss. I went back the next day to the same restaurant, expecting to have more, but there was none. I was promised some for the following day and after partaking of it again, I patiently tried talking in English to the Chinese-speaking chef, endeavoring to decipher his soup's Chinese formula. The soup is not difficult to make, but the *quality* of the melons used, I have discovered, and the proportions of ingredients used in relation to the size of the melon, must be right.

Ingredients for 4 servings

One medium-sized, sun-ripened galia or equivalent green melon weighing around 1 kilo

7–8 cm (3 inches) of fresh root ginger, peeled and roughly chopped; if the ginger shoot is very young, just scrape it rather than peel it

1/2 tablespoon white sugar

The juice of 2 summer oranges (for the base); 'summer' oranges, as they are called in Egypt, are sweet

The juice of 1/2 Lisbon lemon

The Chinese chef in Hong Kong could not exactly describe in English what he meant, but I think he was saying that mandarin (yusefendi) juice, too, is good to use; if mandarins are in season, try the juice of 2, with orange juice

Juice of 2 small green limes

2 pots Greek- or Turkish-style yogurt

Pinch of salt

Juice of 2 more oranges for the completion stage.

Method

To make the base:

1. Carefully cut the melon in half so as not to lose the liquid held inside.
2. Spoon the seeds out into a strainer placed over a blender's container, and press out all the juicy liquid still held around the seeds. Discard the seeds. The melon-seed juice is usually considerable and adds to the soup.
3. Blend the melon-seed juice, ginger, sugar, orange/mandarin, lemon, and lime juices for 10 seconds at liquidizing speed.
4. Scoop out the flesh of the melon into the juice in the blender, starting with the white central creamy flesh down to part—but not all—of the not so sweet green flesh. Too much of the green flesh is not desirable, but use some to give a pale jade-green color to the soup. Blend another 5 seconds.
5. Add yogurt and blend 10 seconds more.

Completion:

1. Stir in the juice of the 2 finishing oranges. This last touch enhances the soup's melon flavor. If possible, let the soup stand for several hours to mature.
2. Chill in the freezer. The soup should be served very cold, just as it is starting to turn to flaky ice—remember this is a soup for a hot summer's day.
3. Serve in either small Chinese bowls, with Chinese poons, or in chilled glass bowls, accompanied by wafer-thin crisp Melba toast, or best of all, crisp toasted 'aysh shami.

Sometimes, in Cairo, we complete our lunch with a splendid dish of several kinds of sliced melon—white, green, and salmon-colored—with cubes of melting ice glistening between the slices, the dish surrounded by bunches of small white iced seedless grapes, sprigs of mint, and halved green limes, ready to squeeze over the melon slices.

Iced Mango Soup

Ambrosial and Aphrodisiac

In Egypt there are many varieties of mangos, such as tay-mur, alphonse, and others, that originated in India. In our Heliopolis garden, we are lucky to have two mango trees, one bearing a small but very sweet mango, the other a deep orange-fleshed fruit from a tree planted by Mohamed more than twenty years ago.

Iced Ambrosial Mango Soup is one of the most exotic foods you can savor, chock-full of the big three antioxidants so favored today: beta carotene, vitamin C, and vitamin E. The idea for the soup came about some years ago, when I was visiting Sidi Abd al-Rahman, on the northern coast of Egypt, for the opening of a new hotel built right on the beach. It was a sweltering July day and the newly installed kitchen had over-chilled their fresh mango juice, which came out iced and flaky. Their small mistake was my delight, and on returning to Cairo I conceived this exotic iced soup.

Ingredients for 4 servings

5 to 6 medium-sized, firm mangos (to produce 8 cups of mango pulp)
2 tablespoons white sugar
1 cup water
The juice of 8–10 freshly squeezed limes, or half a cup of freshly squeezed lemon juice (limes are best)
3 cups yogurt

Method

1. Peel and slice the mangos.
2. Place in blender with sugar, water, and lime juice. Blend for 10 seconds.
3. Tip in the yogurt and blend another 10 seconds.
4. Pour into a thin-sided container and place in the freezing compartment until flaky-iced.
5. Once this flaky ice starts to form, the soup is ready to serve.
6. Serve immediately with thin toasted 'aysh shami or Melba toast.

Note: Use taymur or alphonse mangos if possible. The fruit should be quite firm, not soft, over-ripe, or squashy. If the the mangos are too ripe, the soup will taste as if it had been made with canned mangos, and I can think of nothing worse.

The mango is thought to have first appeared on Earth somewhere in northern India. According to Indian mythology, the tree arose out of the ashes of the daughter of the sun-god. In India to this day, the mango is considered an erotic fruit, and is widely used as an aphrodisiac. When greenish and slightly unripe it is considered to possess its strongest aphrodisiac powers. In India, all-night parties are held at the time of the mango harvest.

Iced Carrot
and Orange Soup

Ambrosial

This is another ravishing summer soup, also classified as 'ambrosial' because of its delectable taste, and just oozing with beta carotene in a form more readily absorbed than plain boiled carrots, which the body apparently has a job digesting when whole. The soup should exude strong carrot and orange flavors.

Ingredients for 4 servings

- 4 sweet or Egyptian summer oranges
- 1 kilogram young carrots, scraped, not peeled, cut into 5-cm (2-inch) pieces (old woody carrots will not work in this recipe)
- 2 medium-sized onions or 4 scallions peeled and quartered
- 2 bay leaves
- 4 medium-sized pearls peeled garlic
- 1 tablespoon white sugar
- A 5-cm (2-inch) piece of peeled ginger, roughly chopped
- 2 teaspoons ground kuzbara (coriander) seed
- Juice of 1 lime
- 1 teaspoon sugar
- The thinly peeled skin of 1 large orange, free of all white pith
- 1 cup light cream
- Very small amount of salt
- A good grinding of freshly ground white pepper
- Handful of whole green kuzbara (coriander) leaves

Method

1. Squeeze the oranges, reserving the juice. Gather up the orange flesh from around the base of the squeezer and add to the juice to accentuate the flavor.
2. Cut the onions into 5-cm (2-inch) pieces. Cover carrots and onions with boiling water and simmer with the bay leaves until almost cooked. Add the orange peel and simmer for another 3 minutes.
3. Discard bay leaves.
4. Throw in the pearls of garlic, sugar, ginger, and kuzbara (coriander) seed. Simmer another five minutes.
5. Remove from the heat and blend to a smooth purée.
6. Stir in the orange and lime juice, sugar, cream, salt, and pepper. Pour mixture into a thin-sided container and place in the freezing compartment of the refrigerator.
7. Freeze until the soup is just turning to icy flakes.
8. Just before serving, sprinkle surface with the green coriander leaves. If too thick, add the juice of one more orange.
9. Serve from a chilled tureen into glass bowls with crisp 'aysh shami, or thin Melba toast. The thin crisp toast acts like the wafers the Italians serve with their wonderful ice creams, helping to keep the palate from numbing, and allowing you to enjoy each spoonful of the soup's carrot flavor.